DOUBLE YOUR 

PROFITS

IN 6 MONTHS OR LESS

Without Stressing About 2x Leads, Cutting Costs, Or Hiking Your Prices – Despite Adverse Market Conditions!

VINEET OJHA

Published by:

Vineet Ojha

vinkr.ojha@gmail.com

1st Edition

September 2020

<u>GRATITUDE</u>

My heartfelt gratitude to my beloved family – my parents, wife & children. I am blessed to have their unconditional support. No words can justify their love, care & cooperation.

I am also grateful to all my teachers, mentors & gurus from whom I have learned – physically or virtually – valuable lessons of life & business.

I am thankful to my fellow authors who helped me making this book more presentable & valuable.

Special mention for Mr. Som Bathla for guiding me on this journey with his vast experience & expertise.

Vineet Ojha
September 14, 2020

"When you do not upgrade your skills; you lose your control over profits. You may increase your volume somehow, but your profitability will not increase."

-Vineet Ojha

PREFACE

For micro, small & medium business owner; profit is not only the need of the business; it is also linked with happiness for yours & your family.

Besides yourself, you spend your profit on your family's comfort, welfare & dreams. You invest your profit for your family's bright future. It is your profit which funds your child's higher education or your family's dream holidays or maybe your new car or house!

A portion of your profit also goes to your employees. It is their bread & butter. Therefore, besides you & your family; your employees & their families also depend on your profit. The happiness & prosperity of all these families is at stake if you don't generate enough profits in your business & keep growing consistently.

Your business profit is an integral part of the country's GDP (Gross Domestic Product) as well. The more you grow your business; the more you are contributing to the economic development of your nation. So, in other words, when you don't grow your business; you let your country down!

Therefore, as a *responsible* businessman, husband, parent, employer & citizen; you are duty-bound to maximize profits in your business consistently.

I was a banker for nearly 17 years. I left a lucrative job from a coveted position to follow my heart. When I got initial success in my business; I was the happiest person on the earth. However, soon, my honeymoon period in business was over and I struggled to run the show. I failed in business/profession. Not once or twice but several times.

Nothing was working for me. I used to read books & watch videos related to business growth. I was overwhelmed with plenty of information and wasn't able to decide which one to follow. Too much information was available with varieties of ideas & methods and it was hard to judge which one will work for me.

Among all the possible way-outs; I wanted only one. The one which was crisp, clear, logical, proven & most suitable to me.

Then, I came across a *wonderful* concept. I was very much convinced that it was the best piece of information I ever had on business growth. I implemented it in my business. And... guess what? It didn't work either. I failed again.

I have learned a lot from my failures in business than from any other thing.

Since my conviction was high on the concept that I had learned; I started pondering why it didn't work for me and why I failed? After spending several weeks, I found out what mistakes I made and how to tweak this concept to suit me at its best. I tried again and this time it worked. Yes! I succeeded!

Then I applied this same concept with other businessmen and they also started getting results. But then, for some businessmen, we faced challenges in its application and it was taking a little longer to get the results.

By & large, small business owners have altogether different mindset & challenges from their counterparts. More so, if they are in the same business for more than 7-8 years, have seen initial growth but now struggle to increase their profits.

In the majority cases, Small business owners do not have a sound & reliable team of qualified & trained people in leadership/sales/managerial roles. They also do not want to come out of their comfort zones.

While working on these challenges I happened to derive a master formula which helps small business owners double their profits in just 6 months or less. When this formula started delivering results; I couldn't stop myself from sharing this with millions of small business owners – like you – across the world.

People have loved this formula so much that from being a 'business coach' earlier; I am now a *'2X Profits Specialist'*.

In this book, you will learn:

a) Simple & powerful steps to double your profits
b) The master formula to double your profits in 6 months or less
c) 2X Profits Strategy Blueprint to double your profits without doubling customers or cutting cost or price hike
d) 2X Profits Strategy Blueprint that works in any trade & market conditions
e) High-impact secrets which you must learn & implement to let the 2X Profits Strategy Blueprint work for you

What's more, you will learn all these in very simple words & lucid language. When I offered it to one of my business friends; he referred to this book as:

'World's Simplest & Most Essential Guide For 2X Profits For Small Business Owners'.

"When your profit is stagnant for the

last few years; your business is in ICU.

Immediately consult a specialist"

-Vineet Ojha

TABLE OF CONTENTS

"If you work hard and yet profits don't increase; it is a signal to change the way you do your business"

-Vineet Ojha

INTRODUCTION

*"At the end of the day,
all that matters is profit."*
– Marley Majcher

This is the story of Neil. He had started his business, for he was highly passionate about it. But today, his passion doesn't help him boost his profits. He works hard still profit is almost stagnant.

Neil is a typical small business owner in the business for 10 years. He had exponential business growth during the initial years, but he could not grow his profits in the last 3-4 years. He tried every possible way on his own & as guided by friends.

Neil also watched informative videos on business growth and implemented the learning, but he couldn't convert it into earning. Few ideas worked & few didn't; and those worked didn't last long. He is now highly frustrated & disappointed.

Neil thinks either he is in the wrong business or maybe he is doing the business more ethically. He has seen several businessmen in his trade grow exponentially by practicing unethical means. Neil doesn't want to do malpractices. He wants profits in the right & ethical way. This makes him even more upset as he cannot find a suitable solution.

Sometimes he feels he should stop doing the business. What is the result of all the hard work that he is putting in his business? He also thinks market conditions are equally responsible for business stagnancy as because of the poor market conditions he cannot generate sufficient profits.

Neil wants to grow. He wants to make it big in the business. He wants to be happy, successful & prosperous. But Neil is not getting any of these. What is worst, his relationship is also at stake because of his stagnant business. He works so hard in his business that he is neither able to spend sufficient quality time with family nor he can spend too much money on family holidays. Their dream luxury car is only a dream – far away from reality.

Though his family has neither raised questions nor shown any dissatisfaction; Neil feels unhappy with the situation. He knows from deep inside that something is missing in the business. He wants to multiply his profits but he feels stuck. And, if this is not enough, he is having multiple routine issues in the business as well. Everyday rises with a new problem in the business. Often, he thinks he is just a fire-fighter in his business!

If you resonate with Neil's story, this is the right book for you. You are going to be immensely benefitted from this book. This book will not only help you to 2X your profits; it will change your life forever.

Let us come back to Neil.

'Ask and it will be given to you; seek and you will find; knock, and the door will be opened to you'.[1]

By thinking about profit, profit & only profit – whole day & night 24X7 – Neil happens to meet 'Mr. Profit' in his dream. Neil feels extremely lucky that he meets 'Mr. Profit' himself. He considers this as his *'Date With Profit'* and narrates his problematic situation to him.

---

[1] *Translation of Matthew 7:7, Sermon on the Mount*

"A business without a path to
profit isn't a business,
it's a hobby."
– Jason Fried

#1: THE FIRST DATE

*"Profit is not something
to add on at the end,
it is something to plan for
in the beginning."
– Unknown*

"Do you have any solution to this?" Neil asked with tears at the corner of the eyes.

"Yes, and No." said Mr. Profit with a mischievous smile.

"For God's sake, no more suspense, please! I am already confused."

"Then be bold & courageous to accept the fact, Neil."

"What fact?"

"Neither market conditions nor prevailing practices are responsible for your business stagnancy. It is only because of the lack of your knowledge & skills to run your business scientifically & intelligently."

"Do you have any idea what are you saying? I am in this business for a decade now. I understand my business very well – in fact, better than anyone else. And the knowledge & skills you are questioning have given me exponential growth earlier. How can you say that I lack the knowledge & skills to run my business? It is ridiculous!" Neil said in a lofty tone.

"The first & foremost lesson you have to learn is whenever you are looking for a solution from anyone – be it your friend, relative or an expert – be ready & open for new ideas. If you stick to your old beliefs; you won't be able to learn anything new. You will keep on looking at the world with the same perspective and will keep on getting the same results again & again. That's not the way to learn & grow. It is nothing but wastage of precious time."

"I am sorry Mr. Profit if I hurt you. I got upset when you questioned my business acumen."

"I know. Neil, if you want to grow, earn more profits & realize dreams of yours & your family, then understand this carefully. This is a very important lesson that will change your perception necessary to learn & grow.

"You are passionate and you know how to start the business and earn profits. Unfortunately, your passion & skill help you only to a certain extent. It rewards you only during the initial years of your business.

"As your business grows, you also need to update your knowledge & skills. You need to learn new skills to make it big. You need to learn how to make a fortune in your business. You need to adopt new thinking and change the way you do your business."

"Is it? But why should I change the ways that have been beneficial for me?

"The basic reason a small business owner either fails in his business or ends up remaining small forever is that he doesn't update his knowledge & skills with time. He keeps on thinking he knows everything. Neither he hires talented people, nor he upgrades his skills. Ultimately, the business suffers.

"Remember, *the force which runs a vehicle differs from the force which starts it.*"

"You sound sensible. I was a fool not to pay attention to it for these many years. But how can I update my knowledge & skills? What exactly I should do? I am more confused & worried now."

"Relax, Neil." Mr. Profit put his hand on Neil's shoulder. "I am here to solve your problems; provided you are equally ready for it."

"Do you think I'm not? I am desperate."

"I can very well understand what is going on in your mind. Remember, *what you focus; expands*. When you keep looking at problems; you will have more. I am sure you are feeling stuck in various problems in almost all the departments of your business, right?"

"Absolutely right. And I don't know what to do. That's why I am asking you for the solution. Do you have the right solution to my problems?"

"I have something even better. I have a 'magical solution'. But... I have to check whether I can share it with you."

"Please don't tease me, Mr. Profit. Tell me, what is it? You know very well that I am heavily upset & fed-up."

"Neil, you need not worry when I am with you. Believe me, the 'magical solution' that I will share with you will give you relief from all your problems. You have been facing them for a long. Leave them as it is for a while and just focus on this 'magical solution'. I repeat. Leave all the problems as it is for a while and focus only on 'magical solution'. Consider it as a mission.

"At the end of the mission, you will have miraculous results. You will find that some of your problems have already vanished, some of them are no more 'problems' to you, and the rest of them you can now solve easily because you always knew how to solve them but you didn't have enough money."

"OMG! Is this really going to be a 'magical solution' for me? Really?"

"Of course, Neil."

"Please tell me what is this 'magical solution'?" Neil asked, leaning forward with wide eyes.

"Ok then listen carefully to the 'magical solution'. *The profound, simplest & only 'magical solution' to your problem is '2X Profits in 6 months or less'*" said Mr. Profit with authority.

"Are you kidding? I expected a practical & logical solution; & not a joke!" Neil said, breathing out, lowering his shoulders & neck.

"Neil, don't be disappointed. I'm serious. Why would I be kidding?" Mr. Profit said in an empathetic voice.

"Here, I'm unable to increase my profits for years and you are telling me to double my profits in the next 6 months only! Isn't it a joke?" Neil said in frustration.

"Have we ever met before? Have I ever taught you how to double your profits? Have you ever followed my advice in any way?" asked Profit in one breath.

"Though we haven't met before, I have tried a lot to follow various ways to increase my profits… but all in vain. I didn't get timely results from any of those. I can't wait for years for profits. In fact, I feel sometimes that they don't understand me at all." Neil's helplessness was evident.

"What all you followed were just ways & means to increase the profits. Those might be wonderful ways, and I agree. But either they were not tailor-made for SMALL BUSINESSES, or there were too many of them confusing you what to follow & what not.

"Once a student needed the spelling of the word 'psychology'. His teacher – rather than sharing the spelling – shared the entire alphabet and said your spelling lies in these letters. Theoretically, the teacher wasn't wrong, but that wasn't the boy wanted.

"This is exactly what is happening with you when you look around for the ways & means of increasing profits quickly – in fact, to double your profits in just a few months. The world is full of information but you don't get what exactly you need in a crisp, clear & simple form. Isn't it?"

"Makes sense. But then, how come few businessmen got the way-out and not me?"

"What would be the percentage of businessmen who double their profits in just a few months? That too when they are in your situation i.e., having a small or medium business for over 7-8 years, are leading a team, and have struggled for years to increase their profits to their satisfaction?"

"Well, if I consider all these aspects then I am sure there will be only a handful of businessmen who succeed in this."

"That's the point, Neil. If you want to get rid of your problems and accelerate your business growth then pay attention to what I am going to share with you. It is not less than a gold mine for you because:

1) I will share only simple & powerful steps (and nothing else) to double your profits in 6 months or less

2) These are tested & proven steps, so you have no reason to doubt

3) You need not double your leads or prospects

4) You need not cut your cost to half

5) I will also share some high-impact secrets which are necessary to follow over & above the steps. Because steps alone won't get you results.

"You might have heard some or many of the steps already. But as I said, there are some high-impact secrets also which you have to learn."

"Wow! That is interesting. I am super excited to know these steps and especially those high-impact secrets which you will reveal." Neil said with sparkling eyes.

"I am so happy to see you excited Neil. Remember, only an enthusiastic person can be on a path of learning." Said Mr. Profit with a smile. "Come prepared tomorrow. We will begin our exciting journey towards '2X Profits in 6 months or less'."

"'2X Profits in 6 months or less'! That is interesting indeed."

"Yes, it is interesting, exciting, and enterprising. If implemented properly, this will turn your fortune forever. You will be out of your financial crunch, your miseries, your pains because of lesser profits, and will have a wonderful life full of time & money. You will also have health, wealth, relations & respect with this. So, don't underestimate it and follow what I say. See you tomorrow."

"That is outstanding! But why tomorrow? Why not right now?"

"Patience, dear Neil, patience. Do you want me to be as overwhelming as all the other information you were absorbing earlier?"

"Of course not."

"Then do what I say. Take a sound sleep. I will see you tomorrow. And remember, you can find me only if you are eager to see me. Bye-bye."

*"Profit is the ignition system
of our economic engine."
– Charles Sawyer*

WHAT WE LEARNED:

- Market conditions or prevailing practices are not responsible for business stagnancy
- You need to update your knowledge & skills with your business's growth
- The force which runs a vehicle differs from the force which starts it
- What you focus; expands. So, decide where you want to focus – on problems or solutions?
- The profound, simplest & only 'magical solution' to the problems (similar to that of Neil) is '2X Profits in 6 months or less'
- There are some simple & powerful steps and few high-impact secrets to having '2X Profits in 6 months or less'

#2: RULE OF 2-3-4

"Our goals can only be reached through the vehicle of a plan. There is no other route to success."
– Pablo Picasso

As Neil was about to get the secrets for '2X Profits in 6 months or less'; he was highly excited to meet Mr. Profit the next day (night, to be precise). In fact, he was so excited that he went to bed way early than usual. He kept on thinking about meeting Mr. Profit while going to sleep. More & more he thought about it, more desperate he became to meet him.

"Hey, Neil! I am glad that you found me. Thank you."

"Hello, Mr. Profit. Please don't say thanks to me. In fact, I am thankful to you for allowing me to meet you. I feel highly honored & the chosen one. Thank you."

"Haha... the chosen one! You know what? I am equally desperate to meet someone like you. I rarely find people genuinely interested in me or, you can say, are eager to have me."

"Sorry to say, but I don't agree. Why a businessman will not be eager to have you? Probably, you are the very basic reason of his doing business. Isn't it?"

"Yes, it is. But most of them either take unethical ways to have me or they don't care enough once they have me. Who would like to be with such a person, Neil?"

"Hmmm. You are right. So, what is your advice for me? I am eager to know."

"Sure, I will tell you that in a while. But before we begin, let me clarify one thing. Since now we are in good rapport; I will speak to-the-point. Hope you won't mind that."

"Mind? I will love that. But... I am confused about why you insist on having '2X profits in 6 months or less'? Why not 10X profits in 3-5 years? Or why not 2X profits in 4 or 12 months? I mean... you are 'the Profit'. Everything is possible for you. Isn't it? Then why you insist on this only?"

"That's an intelligent question, Neil. My experience says small business owners –

especially stuck in your situation – must start with '2X Profits in 6 months or less'. Because:

1) It is exciting & easily doable

2) It requires minimum steps

3) It generates reasonably quick results

4) It is not overwhelming

5) It is not haphazard

6) it is designed in a convincing & logical manner for you to have your continued faith

"You are right that I can tell you ways to 10X your profits in 3-5 years, but that would be highly overwhelming & in most cases unbelievable. When you do not have unquestionable continued faith in something; you show a lack of consistency & intensity in your efforts. As a result, you don't get the desired outcome.

"I can also tell you how to double your profit in 4 months or even in 2 months, but that either won't be convincing for you or it won't be a repeatable model. See, all these are a kind of 'good to have' but not suitable for beginners like you. For a small business owner like you, the best way to begin is '2X Profits in 6 months or less'.

"Also, I will teach you these steps in such a way that you can repeat the entire process even twice or thrice! Doesn't it make sense?"

"Of course! I am glad to see how much you care for me. One more question. Is this applicable to all or just me?"

"Good question. The master formula I will reveal applies to those businessmen who meet ALL the below criteria:

1) Small business owners

2) Who are traders, manufacturers, distributors, service providers, or in similar businesses

3) Who are in the businesses for over 7-8 years

4) Who have seen exponential growth during the initial period of their businesses

5) Who feel their business growth is stagnant since the last 2-3 years or more

6) Who have employees under them i.e., they have a team to lead

7) Where all decision-makers are committed for '2X Profits in 6 months or less' i.e., the proprietor or all partners/directors must be 100% committed to having this

Wherever you have any doubt (as to its applicability) you can clarify with me then & there."

"Thanks. For whom this is not applicable?"

"This is not applicable for solopreneurs, professionals, and self-employed. This is also not applicable to those businessmen who don't meet even a single criterion as mentioned above. Such businessmen need to follow a different model & approach. Therefore, it would be wise not to keep them in mind at present."

"Got it. Thanks for the clarity, Mr. Profit."

"You're welcome. Let me begin with the basic principles of '2X Profits in 6 months or less':

1) You must have only simple & bare minimum steps for 2X Profits

2) These steps must not be overwhelming to you otherwise you will be lost and will not be inclined to follow them

3) There is a difference between building an empire and having 2X Profits. When your immediate goal is to build an empire; you need to follow a series of steps and that's an altogether different story. But when your immediate goal is '2X Profits in 6 months or less'; then your approach will be totally different. Therefore, keeping our immediate goal in mind, I will share those precise points only.

"This is very, very important. Most businessmen make a mistake here."

"How? I mean, how most businessmen make a mistake here?"

"Most businessmen just want to have 'growth'. They don't know exactly how much growth and in which direction? Do they want higher turnover, more revenue, more sales, more brand loyalty?

What? How much? By when? And when asked, they all want everything maximum.

"That is not the right approach. You must have a precise understanding & strategic approach for the desired growth. Mere going in any direction and then getting distracted won't get you the required milestone."

"You are right. Whichever models I have referred so far to double my profits have been overwhelming for me. I feel there is so much to do and just after a couple of days, I lose my motivation. I really need those precise steps for 2X Profits."

"Correct. The steps I will share with you are nothing less than *Golden Nugget*."

"Yes, I completely understand. I am ready & eager to have them."

"Great. The first thing you have to learn is the *'Rule of 2-3-4'.*"

"Rule of 2-3-4?"

"Yes. 'Rule of 2-3-4'. I have formed this rule to let you remember these golden nuggets in an easier and non-forgettable way. This is what 'Rule of 2-3-4' stands for:

2 –   2X Profits

3 –   3 Secrets

4 –   4 Strategies

"This simply means: *To have '2X Profits in 6 months or less'; there are 3 secrets and 4 strategies.* 2-3-4. Easy, isn't it?"

"Yes, easy & equally interesting."

"Good. We have enough for the day. See you tomorrow with more details. Bye Neil."

"Hey! Why don't you finish it today itself?"

"Remember, what I said yesterday?   Patience, Neil, patience. Bye…"

"The engine which drives enterprise is not thrift, but profit."
– John Maynard Keynes

<u>**WHAT WE LEARNED:**</u>

- Having '2X Profits in 6 months or less' is to be the first step to business growth for various reasons
- The master formula for '2X Profits in 6 months or less' is applicable for small business owners who meet certain criteria (as mentioned)
- This does not apply to solopreneurs & professionals
- This is also not applicable to those businessmen who do not meet even a single criterion (as mentioned)
- Remember the 'Rule of 2-3-4' i.e., for 2X profits there are 3 secrets and 4 strategies

<u>#3: PREPARING YOURSELF</u>

*"Once your mindset changes,
everything on the outside
will change along with it."
– Steve Maraboli*

"As I said earlier, there are 3 secrets to have '2X Profits in 6 months or less' and now I will reveal these high-impact secrets to you, one by one.

"Without these secrets; your strategies won't fetch you any result. Most of the businessmen do not know this. They just follow something said by someone and eventually get disappointed. Remember: *'Secrets first; strategies second'.*

"Secrets are the base of your pizza. You can't have just toppings without the base. In other words, success – your topping – has no place without the base of these high-impact secrets."

"Superb! So, what is the first secret to have '2X Profits in 6 months or less'?"

"Secret # 1 to have '2X Profits in 6 months or less' is having a proper **mindset**."

"Mindset?"

"Yes. Mindset is the root of all your triumphs. No war is won without having a proper mindset. Almost every sport is first considered being a mind game & then a physical game. Attracting your date or profit is a game & war. You have to have the correct mindset else you won't achieve what you want.

"Mindset helps you to take the proper decision, remain motivated, chose the right path, be on track, look from a different perspective, gamify & enjoy your journey, avoid stress, remain happy, face adversity, sustain rejection/failure... and what not!

"Therefore, if you want '2X Profits in 6 months or less', you must have a proper mindset. Without it, you would just be experimenting with your business with no serious gains."

"I am already motivated to have the correct mindset for my '2X Profits in 6 months or less'. What exactly I need to do to have it?"

"Good question, Neil. What all you need to do for having the right mindset for '2X Profits in 6 months or less' is this:

SELF BELIEF

"Once there lived two friends in a village. Both were equal in talent, knowledge & personality. Both had similar financial conditions. Both started doing a job in a nearby city. Gradually, both started their small businesses. After a few months, one expanded the business a little whereas the other didn't. He was afraid of losing money.

"The first one further expanded the business, but the other one remained as it is. For him, he was not yet ready for the market conditions. He thought he had no prior experience of handling this much business. So, what if he fails? Over the period, the one who expanded got very rich & successful. He had all the luxuries and huge respect in society. Whereas the one who didn't expand was living an ordinary life. What do you think was the key difference between them?"

"Risk-taking ability?"

"Absolutely. And how does one increase his risk-taking ability? By having a high self-belief. I don't say you take blind risks. No. But you must always have a high self-belief. Some people also consider this as self-confidence. You need to have faith in yourself.   You need to believe that YOU CAN. Believe that you have got enormous potential."

[Pic: 3.1]

"What if in your story the friend who expanded fails in his attempt?"

"Do you think he didn't? He failed several times. But he had a high self-belief that HE CAN.   He never accepted the circumstances and kept trying.   If one way didn't produce results, he changed & tried another way. If he felt he lacked some skills, he learned them.   Eventually, he succeeded because of his high self-belief.

"In business, you won't have a red-carpet journey for success. You may have to struggle sometimes. You may have to find your way through the dark.

But if you have a high self-belief, you can easily pass all these adverse situations."

"But is it not foolishness to have high self-belief when you don't have skills?"

"Skills can be learned. I already said don't take risks blindly. But when you are sure that you are following the correct path or you are following a learned person, then surrender him and do what he says with 100% self-belief. Generally, self-belief has a major impact on these areas:

1) It forces you to use your full potential. Sometimes even enhances your potential
2) It allows you to learn new skills and enhance your capabilities
3) It gives you the confidence to face the worst
4) It increases your risk-taking ability
5) Eventually, you grab opportunities when others fail to recognize

"If a businessman doesn't have the above qualities, do you think he can ever succeed?"

"No way. But what if he still fails?"

"Success is never guaranteed. No one has seen the future. There are many things which we can't foresee and which are not in our control. But that doesn't mean we should stop growing.

"A bird flies high in the sky, not because she considers the sky friendly but because she trusts her wings and believes in herself. The speed of a deer is much faster than a tiger. But eventually, he is caught by the tiger because the deer feels he can't run faster than the tiger, whereas the tiger believes he can catch the deer.

"*We get the result according to our thoughts & beliefs.* This is how self-belief can affect one's life."

"Amazing!"

"Believe you can…
and you are halfway there."
– Theodore Roosevelt

STAY COMMITTED

"Next step is having a non-compromised goal of '2X Profits in 6 months or less'. Non-compromised means you won't change your goal – come what may. The goal must always be fixed. You can be flexible in your approaches. You can be flexible in ways with which you will achieve the goal, but not the goal itself. The goal has to be fixed until achieved.

"This is required because situations may keep on changing every now & then. If you are not having a definite or fixed goal, you will keep on shuffling your direction and will land nowhere.

"Even if you don't get initial success in the business, don't give up. Even if you find your friends, relatives, or fellow businessmen laughing at you or criticize you; don't give up.

"Once the goal is fixed then you have to stay committed to making all the efforts it needs. Even if you have to come out of your comfort zone; don't hesitate – believe me, success is often found outside the comfort zone. Often, *success is not what you get but what you become in getting*."

"No matter how many mistakes you make or how slow you progress. You're still way ahead of everyone who isn't trying."
-Tony Robbins

VISUALIZE DAILY

"You are not alone in this world. Many forces affect your outcome. You have to incorporate certain rituals to make the universe work for you.

"Many people refer to the universe with different names e.g., nature, supreme power, God, etc. That is ok. Whatever you believe in; use that divine power/force to support you in your triumph. How wonderful it would be when your dedicated efforts are even favored by the universe!

"The first such ritual is to visualize daily. You have to daily visualize yourself achieving your goal. I believe you know what I mean by visualizing. Don't you?"

"Yes. I have read somewhere that visualization means you have to sit in a calm place, close your eyes, take a couple of deep breaths, and then see the images in your mental screen."

"That's wonderful. Better if images are moving and not still. In other words, instead of pictures, try to see the movie. Make an imaginary movie that you have already achieved your goal of 2X Profits in less than 6 months and see how happy you are, its positive impact on your business, yours fulfilling your dreams, your happy family... etc.

"Add as many details as you can. Better, if you can add some sound/audio as well. That will enhance your experience. In short, make the movie as wonderful & realistic as you can. See this movie on your mental screen at least twice a day – once just after you wake-up in the morning and once when you are about to sleep.

"The next ritual is to keep your goal in your mind, 24X7. Rather than ritual, some people prefer to name this task as 'obsession'. Doesn't matter. Whatever you may call it. The essence is clear that you have to wake-up, sleep, walk, talk, eat, breathe, work only & only with your goal in mind i.e., having '2X Profits in 6 months or less'.

"These rituals will not only keep you focused & motivated; they will also make things happen for you. You will notice you are getting help unexpectedly. You will have ideas suddenly. You will get a flood of opportunities suddenly. Keep on doing this daily and your life will be changed forever."

"Growth is never by mere chance; It is the result of forces working together."
-James Cash Penny

<u>**WHAT WE LEARNED:**</u>

- Secrets first; strategies second
- The first secret of Rule 2-3-4 is to have the correct mindset
- There is an altogether different mindset of a successful or growing entrepreneur vs a stuck one. We need to have the right mindset to move forward, else, nothing is going to work
- Self-Belief plays a vital role in a businessman's growth. It not only helps to have high confidence but also helps to have desired risk-taking ability
- Success is not guaranteed. That doesn't mean we should stop growing
- We need to stay committed towards our aim of having 2X Profits in 6 months or less
- Success is not what you get but what you become in getting.
- To make things happen for us and to have universal power in our favor, we need to daily visualize that we've achieved our goal. This is very important to have miracles in our life & business
- Keep your goal in mind 24X7. You will notice you are getting help in unexpected ways

#4: THE MOST PRECIOUS THING

"Successful and unsuccessful people do not vary greatly in their abilities. They vary in their desire to reach their potential."
-John Maxwell

"The second secret to having '2X Profits in 6 months or less' is the **focus**. Not time, but the focus is the most precious thing in the world. If you are not focused, you lose your time as well.

"Focus is the power to give your energy proper direction. Focus is the art of not getting distracted. Focus ensures that you remember your goals pretty well. Focus gives you the reason to get up in the morning & work hard for your goals.

"Ask any sportsman the secret of his success and he will tell you the importance of focus. Ask any successful person about the reasons he is successful and his entire talk will be around remaining focused. Ask any student how he got good grades and he will tell you the story of how focused he was in his studies."

UNDIVIDED ATTENTION

"You need to have your undivided attention on 2X Profits otherwise you are unlikely to get it. At least you have to do it for the next 6 months if not forever. Make sure whenever you are working on your business; you remain totally focused. You need to be away from all kinds of distractions.

"While passing through a bridge in America, Swami Vivekananda saw some boys were trying to shoot eggshells that were floating in the water but they missed every time they shoot. After some time, Swamiji went close to the boys and asked for the gun. The boys hesitated but then gave the gun to Swamiji. Swamiji fired 12 times and every time he fired, he hit eggshells. Boys were surprised to see a monk was shooting with such great precision!

"Inquisitive boys asked, 'how were you able to do this'? Swamiji replied, *'whatever you are doing, put your whole mind to it. If you are shooting, then your mind should be only on the target. Only then you will be able to do this. Once you learn to focus your mind on target, then you will never miss it'*.

"Basis, if you remain focused on your approach and have undivided attention on your goal, you are most likely to win."

MAKE THIS YOUR #1 PRIORITY

"Make '2X Profits in 6 months or less' your topmost priority for the next 6 months. I know many businessmen are having multiple businesses. If you want to make '2X Profits in 6 months or less' then your topmost priority has to be this particular business only. Believe me, you won't get results otherwise.

"If you are working on multiple items simultaneously, your energy gets divided. For getting this much result at this speed, you need to have your entire energy focused on one thing only. If you are serious about having '2X Profits in 6 months or less' than you have to seek it much more than any other damn thing.

"You can't treat it the same as other 100 things in your mind. Everything else should be secondary to this. You may have to postpone your holidays or you may have to defer watching your favorite movies or game, but that's the price you have to pay. If you are not willing to pay that price, you are unlikely to get it."

*"Good things happen when
you set your priorities straight."*
-Scott Caan

ALL DECISIONS TO BE IN ALIGNMENT

"This is obvious. When you have '2X Profits in 6 months or less' your topmost priority and you are giving your undivided attention to it than by default, all your decisions will be based on the same focused philosophy only.

"However, for the slightest chance, if you get distracted from your focused approach, this technique will have a check on it:

"Verify your each & every decision whether it is taken keeping your focus & priority intact or not? e.g., your close friend asks you to go for an outing. You haven't been there for long, feel tired & would love to take an abrupt break. Basis, you agree.

"Now, check whether your decision (of agreeing for an outing) is passing the criteria of your focus & priority? If yes, then go ahead with your decision, and, if no, then you have to change your decision.

"Sometimes we may get distracted. We get fascinated with something or we get an urge of doing something. Many forces test us. We realize it very late that it was nothing but a distraction. The practice I explained will be extremely helpful in all such times."

FOCUSED ACTIONS

"When we talk about focus; it inevitably includes actions. One should expect nothing in the world without acting first. We have seen so many businessmen who are very well aware of everything but even then, they fail because either they don't take the right action at the right time or they lack focus on their actions. In other words, they take half-hearted actions.

"Concentrated action is the key to success. Your actions must also show consistency when required. Scattered actions are nothing but wastage of resources. Better one should avoid it. Therefore, your focus is to be followed with timely focused actions.

"Now I think you are convinced with the importance of remaining focused. Aren't you?"

"Yes, indeed. And I must admit you are explaining to me in the simplest yet convincing manner. Thank you so much, Mr. Profit."

"Productivity is never an accident. It is always the result of a commitment to excellence, intelligent planning, and focused effort."
-Paul J Meyer

<u>**WHAT WE LEARNED:**</u>

- The second secret to having '2X Profits in 6 months or less' is focus
- Focus is the most precious element in this world, not even time, because if you lose focus; you also lose time
- You have to pay undivided attention to your business and especially to your growth strategies. If you have multiple things on your hands then your energy gets divided. As it is rightly said 'how you eat an elephant?' 'One piece at a time'
- Having '2X Profits in 6 months or less' must be your # 1 priority at least for the next 6 months. If you give it the same importance as 100 other things in your mind; it's not going to work
- Your all decisions in business to be in alignment with your goal of having '2X Profits in 6 months or less'. Make it a mission
- Focused action is the next key to get the desired results. Everything is wasted if proper actions are not taken
- Ideas are worthless, if not act upon

#5: CREATING TIME

"Focus on being productive;
instead of busy."
-Tim Ferriss

"The secret I will reveal to you now is though last in the sequence but truly a secret for many. Many businessmen do not know how to deal with it. Would you like to know what is it?"

"Of course. Please tell me what it is."

"Ok. Since you are convinced that you are whole-heartedly going for '2X Profits in 6 months or less'; what question comes to your mind when you constantly think about it?"

"Honestly, I am so excited to implement this learning in my business that I don't even think about obstacles. But there is one thing which comes to my mind whenever I think of this."

"And, what is that?"

"Do I have sufficient time to implement these learning? I mean, I remain so occupied in my business that I cannot figure out when I will find time for all these without letting my routine business suffer. There is no meaning of working about the future by spoiling the present. I am sorry to say this, but this comes to my mind, honestly."

"Wonderful. That is exactly what our secret is all about. I know the biggest obstacle is not a lack of knowledge, but a lack of time or strategy.

"Therefore, the third secret is 'Create Time'. I don't say manage your time. I say 'create time'. The owner of the business must be available for the business. Note my words carefully. I am saying he should be available for 'business' – not for operations.

"One of the major drawbacks of small business owners – like you – is that they are overloaded with work in the business as if they are the sole worker there. They hardly enjoy a holiday without getting a call from their businesses. They hardly get time for their family. Sometimes it feels what the team is doing then?

"If you don't have time even for your important tasks; how will you work on '2X Profits in 6 months or less'? That's why you need to work on these areas:

PRODUCTIVITY

"One must diligently work to increase one's productivity. You are capable of doing more in lesser time, but somehow you are not doing it. Most of you do not have even your task-list ready. The first thing you should do is to prepare your task-list (or to-do list).

"This must be ready with you a day in advance i.e., by the time you leave your office for the day, you should be having your next day's to-do list ready with you. It is not that much difficult as it appears. The meticulous practice of few weeks makes it very easy forever.

"If you wonder how to-do list is to be prepared or what to write in the list, then pay attention to this:

1) **Basis Priority/Urgency**: One way of making a to-do list is to prepare basis priority or urgency. That means what is at the priority is to be done first. Then a lesser priority task and so on. What is of the least priority/urgency; will appear at the bottom of the list.

2) **Basis Importance**: The to-do list can also be prepared basis what is more important i.e., a particular task may not be a priority or

urgent at this moment but it is important e.g., guiding a new staff when you have other tasks on hand. This may seem lesser priority item or not-so-urgent, but it is important. Another such example is production planning for next month. It is important but not urgent on the 20th of the month.

3) **Basis Profitability**: You can also make your to-do list based on which task will earn you profit/revenue and which won't. Chose to do those tasks first which are directly linked with profits and leave the rest.   If time permits, you can then work on tasks that are not liked with profits.

"So, these were various examples of how to make a to-do list. To begin with, start with the first method for a month. In the second month, go for the second one, and in the third month go for the third one. By then you will have a broad idea of how things have improved and how you should move ahead.   You can pick your style from thereon.

"Another best way to enhance your productivity is to come office early. You must come to your office for one hour before regular hours begin for your staff. During this extra one hour, the first rule is not to check your email or phone. Dedicate this one hour in planning for the day. Since you have your to-do list ready, ponder on the tasks mentioned.

"You can also use this golden hour for thinking about something new or innovative. You also have the option to think about how you can leave early from office (not once or twice but as a routine). Once found, this will give you the much-needed time for yourself & family. This will also keep you stress-free and will be useful in '2X Profits in 6 months or less' if needed.

"Making a to-do list or coming office early are only a few small steps to increase your productivity. There are many more things which can help you in this area. But as said earlier, I am sharing only the bare minimum things with you at present, so I am not touching other points. You can refer & learn on your own later, say after 6 months."

"Productivity is not just doing more, it is about creating more impact with less work."
-Unknown

GET OVER FROM ROUTINE OPERATIONS

"Majority small businessmen remain so occupied in their routine operations that it is hard to figure out whether they are the owners or most obedient employees of their businesses? Jokes apart, it is sad to see them like this. This was good during the early stage of your business but not now. Unless you are free from operations, how can you be creative or think of expanding your business further?

"You need to understand the difference between *'business'* and *'busy-ness'*. Unfortunately, most Small business owners are only busy in the business. An outsider when see you working so hard will believe that you are earning a fortune, but only you know the reality.

"Therefore, make it a target that you will get over from your routine operations in a fortnight (or, in a month, maximum, if you are more laborious). How? Take a pen-n-paper. First, write down all the tasks which keep you occupied the whole day in business. Then, write down vertically the names of your core employees (key team members/managers/supervisors) and then horizontally write their duties/tasks against their names. Check whether anyone has lesser work or anyone works more than others. Distribute the tasks evenly (including tasks you were doing).

"Do not listen to your employees at present. They may paint an altogether different picture. Use your experience and instruct them. If needed, be with them on their job and show them how the task can be completed quickly.

"This entire exercise may take several days – depending upon your business and number of key employees – but believe me once done scientifically, it will smoothen your operations and reduce your burden.

"If required, you may also consider hiring someone for a particular task or a bunch of tasks. Don't hesitate because this is a genuine & structured business requirement.

"By not hiring, you won't save any cost. Think like this: If hiring someone gets you a few hours free, then how much more productive/useful you can be for your business in those hours? People say time can't be bought. But, if you can create more free time for you by paying a few bucks, it's a wise deal."

DELEGATION

"Getting work done is art. Like leadership, it is a must-have skill for a businessman. One who doesn't master the art of delegation; cannot be an effective leader. Delegation is also an integral part of your freedom if you are stuck in operations.

"However, most of the Small business owners do not know how to perfectly delegate. Some of them fear delegating important tasks because they think the other person won't be able to do it as good as they themselves do. Some others fear, what if they do not complete the task in a given time? Some people also think it will be a wastage of time if they have to first teach them how to do because by the time they will teach, they themselves will complete so there is no point in delegating.

"All these doubts & fears are baseless. It is only a lack of delegation skills and nothing else. Delegation is a 5 steps process[2]:

1)   I Do; You See

2)   We Do

3)   You Do; I See

4)   You Do

5)   Support & Review

---

[2] *Delegation Process is formed basis the contents from: https://workmonger.com/management-and-delegation/*

"Step (1) above refers that first, you have to do the task yourself and let your employee have a look at it. Then, in step (2) you both do it jointly i.e., depending upon the task you can share the task or do it turn by turn. Thereafter, step (3) indicates that now let your employee do the task and you watch him. This way, you can guide him where he is making a mistake, so he learns then & there. (4) Once he is comfortable and starts doing a task satisfactorily; then let him do it independently. (5) However, don't forget to provide your support whenever needed. Being a vigilant leader, don't wait for him to ask for it; monitor his progress and offer your support whenever you feel necessary.

"This will ensure that they complete the task within the timeline. Otherwise, you will come to know only at the end that the task is incomplete and then you might not have any way-out but suffer.

"By following this model, you will be a master of delegation and will have enough time in spare. This will take some time but that will be an investment of time & energy which will give your sweet fruits for a long period.

"So, how are you feeling dear Neil?"

"I am feeling blessed at present. Highly blessed that I have you to teach me all these. I could have never thought of these aspects on my own and God knows how much time & money I would have wasted otherwise on various other sources to get the solution. Thanks again, Mr. Profit."

"Oh, c'mon Neil. I am extremely happy to share this with you. Hope you will use it in your business."

"Of course. I am eager to do so at the earliest possible. Only waiting to first listen to you completely before taking any action. I don't want to do things haphazardly."

"That's lovely. Remember, *learn to work 'on' the business; not 'in' the business.* Bye for now, Neil. See you again tomorrow."

"Bye-bye."

"Productivity is less about what you do with your time, and more about how you run your mind."
-Robin Sharma

<u>**WHAT WE LEARNED:**</u>

- The final secret to have '2X Profits in 6 months or less' is to create time
- Time is to be 'created' because you are not going to find it any other way. You have to create it from what you have. Every minute saved is a minute created
- There is no point in learning the secrets & strategies of '2X Profits in 6 months or less' if you don't have time to implement them
- There is no point either in having '2X Profits in 6 months or less' if you don't have sufficient time for yourself, your family & your business
- You need to be more productive. There is a huge difference between being busy & being productive
- Do more in less. Create more impact doing the same work in lesser time. Learn to do things differently
- To create time, most crucial is to get rid of your routine business operations. These are either clerical tasks or non-revenue generating tasks. Avoid doing them personally. Rather, invest your time in business growth because no one else will do it for you
- Learn to delegate. You can't grow if you don't delegate smartly. Once you identify which tasks are to be delegated and to whom, then follow 5 step process of delegation
- Learn to work 'on' the business; not 'in' the business

#6: STRATEGY BLUEPRINT

"A vision without a strategy remains an illusion."
-Lee Bolman

"Now I am presenting to you the heart of the '2X Profits in 6 months or less'. It is called the *2X Profits Strategy Blueprint.*

"You need to understand this *2X Profits Strategy Blueprint* pretty well. If you master this, it will change the way you think about your business. New possibilities will get opened up to you for your '2X Profits in 6 months or less'.

"Before I present the *2X Profits Strategy Blueprint;* let me ask you something. What do you think you should do to have '2X Profits in 6 months or less'? Tell me."

"It's quite simple. I have to double my sales."

"Good. And what will you do to double your sales?"

"To double my sales, I need to double my customers. But that's the actual problem. How can I double my customers in just 6 months? Frankly, you just have to say only whereas I have to do it practically."

"Haha... I had expected this exact answer at this point. *What if I say you can double your profits without doubling your customers?* Will you believe it?"

"Honestly, it is hard to believe. But... Let me think... Yes, got it! You mean to say I should work on my cost as well. So, theoretically, by increasing my customers 50% and simultaneously reducing my cost by 50% I can double my profit. Isn't it? But mind you, this is just a theory, ok?"

"I had expected this as well. *What if I tell you that you can double your profits without doubling your customers and without cutting even a penny in your cost?* Will you believe it?"

"Are you kidding or what? That is impossible. Even a kid can tell that you aren't serious."

"That's the entire game, Neil. Unfortunately, most Small business owners do not write business figures on paper by themselves. They have an 'idea' about their figures, but they don't have the 'exact picture' in black & white. It is a must. How will you plan for growth when you do not know where to put your energy? And how much?

"Having everything on paper gives better clarity. It not only helps you to remember well, but it also enhances your decision-making power. That's why *2X Profits Strategy Blueprint* is of vital importance."

"That's cool, but who likes to play with figures? At least not we businessmen." Said Neil, smiling.

"I will present the *2X Profits Strategy Blueprint* to you in such a simple way that it will be very easy for you to remember it forever.

"This is the *2X Profits Strategy Blueprint* for having '2X Profits in 6 months or less'. Look at the below table carefully:

No.	Particular	Figure
Ⓐ	Number of Leads	5,000
Ⓑ	Lead Conversion Ratio	20%
C	Number of Customers (A X B)	1,000
Ⓓ	Average Sales Per Customer	50
E	Total Sales (C X D)	50,000
Ⓕ	Cost of Per Unit Sold	20
G	Total Cost of Goods Sold (F X C)	20,000
Ⓗ	Fixed Cost	10,000
I	**PROFIT** (E – G – H)	**20,000**

Figures in USD except numbers in rows A & C

[Table 6.1 : PROFIT CALCULATOR]

"Very carefully I am not using any jargon here so that you can understand it even if you are not a financial person. Any businessman will understand this simple table. Isn't it?"

"Yes, of course. It is pretty simple & straight forward. But this is just a table. Where is the strategy?"

"When will you learn to have patience, Neil?"

"Sorry. I am so eager to learn the strategy so... you know..."

"There are total 9 rows with figures in the table and I have labeled them from A to I. Interestingly, out of these 9 rows, 5 are under your control viz A, B, D, F and H. Rest 4 (i.e., C, E, G and I) are just the product or calculation based on those 5 rows. In other words, rows that are not encircled depend on other rows that are encircled. So, technically, you can work on these five rows A, B, D, F, and H to increase/decrease your profits.

"This means, instead of working just on increasing Customers, now you have below mentioned 5 areas with help of which you can increase your profits:

1) Number of Leads

2) Lead Conversion Ratio

3) Average Sales Per Customer

4) Cost Per Unit Sold (variable cost)

5) Fixed Cost

"Amazing! When I think of doubling the number of customers, it appears to be a daunting task but when I think in terms of leads, conversion ratio, sales per customer, cost, etc. it releases the pressure to some extent. But I am not clear how exactly I will use these factors for my 2X Profits. Also, 2X Profits still looks impossible."

"You have not seen the magic yet, Neil. What I will show you now will blow your mind completely. Right now, what looks 'impossible' will be felt 'quite simple & easily doable' and that's my promise to you. You can't imagine how simple I will make it for you."

"I don't think so. Where is the possibility now to make it simpler? You must be exaggerating Mr. Profit."

"Ok. I am challenging you. If I do not make this 'quite simple & easily doable' for you in the next few minutes, I am ready to do whatever you say. And if I succeed, then you have to do whatever I say. Do you agree, Neil?"

"Challenge accepted. I am damn sure I will win. There is nothing you can do here."

"Ok then. First, it is a myth that you can't double your customers in 6 months or you can't work 100% on all the five areas mentioned above because you can very well do it and it is proven several times in almost all the trades & businesses.

"But how about improving only 15% in each of these five areas? I am sure you agree that 15% improvement is not a daunting task but just stretching a little. If you work hard for it, can't you improve just 15% in any given areas of the business? Just 15%?"

"Well… you know… actually… 15% improvement is somehow seeming possible – especially when I have a master like you. But what will it give? I want a 100% profit increase and not just a 15% improvement. I am sure you know what I am talking about!"

"Great. I know. Now, look at the same table again, with just – and just – 15% improvement in each of those 5 areas:

<u>Note</u>: As we improve, every value in the below table will not increase. Take an example of cost. When we say that we have improved or gone better, the cost will increase or decrease? It will decrease. Because an increase in cost is not an improvement; it's the other way. Therefore, in the below table, values of two rows F & H (which are costs) will reduce, and the values of the other three rows i.e., A, B & D will increase.

No.	Particular	Figure	% Imp*	Revised Figure
(A)	Number of Leads	5,000	15%	5,750
(B)	Lead Conversion Ratio	20%	15%	23%
C	Number of Customers (A X B)	1,000		1,322
(D)	Average Sales Per Customer	50	15%	57.50
E	Total Sales (C X D)	50,000		76,015
(F)	Cost of Per Unit Sold	20	15%	17
G	Total Cost of Goods Sold (F X C)	20,000		22,474
(H)	Fixed Cost	10,000	15%	8,500
I	**PROFIT** (E – G – H)	**20,000**	**125%**	**45,041**

*Imp = Improvement
Figures in USD except numbers in rows A & C

[Table 6.2 : 2X PROFITS STRATEGY BLUE PRINT]

"What? 125% increase in profits!! With just a 15% improvement!! This is insane!! Not possible. You must have made some error in the calculation."

"It is a factual calculation, Neil. Do it yourself to believe."

"Unbelievable. How is it possible to have a 125% increase with just 15% improvement?"

"That's the magic I was talking about. And that is why having such figures on paper is very much important for a businessman. Hasn't this opened new possibilities for you?"

"Yes. I am amazed. This is exceptional!"

"We were talking about having 2X Profits i.e., a 100% increase in profits whereas we got a 125% increase. And that too with just a 15% improvement in certain areas of our business. Isn't it incredible?"

"Please don't ask me anything right now. I am yet to recover from the pleasant shock you've given to me. I need some time, please."

"Haha… I know. This happens with most of the businessmen when the first time they learn this *2X Profits Strategy Blueprint* in this simplest way."

"I am totally convinced with this *2X Profits Strategy Blueprint* and I fully agree that it is 'quite simple & easily doable.' I am more than happy to lose the challenge to you. Because what I got by losing is much more valuable for me than anything else at this moment. This is a lifelong lesson and will definitely change my business forever."

"This is simple math and nothing else. Just a fresh perspective to look at your business."

"I can't thank you enough for this, Mr. Profit."

"Any question so far, Neil?"

"Does this apply to every business in the same way?"

"Good question. This is just an example. Your actual figures will differ. But the strategy & formula will remain the same for all. However, there will be some adjustments in % distribution of cost, etc. depending upon your business type i.e., manufacturers, traders, service provides, etc. and also will differ with the exact commodity you deal with. But that will only vary a few % here-n-there. The core concept will remain the same. I am sure you are getting what I am saying."

"Yes. My friends will be delighted to learn this."

"Yes. But before teaching them this *2X Profits Strategy Blueprint*; I want you to implement this first. And once you get results; tell at least three close friends of yours to implement this in their businesses as well. This is what you have to do for losing the challenge to me. Will you do it, Neil?"

"How sweet of you! I would love to do it, Mr. Profit. I have to just improve 15% in 5 areas, that's it!"

"Yes. Good to see you upbeat for taking action. But let me clarify here something. 15% is just an example I've shown here. This doesn't mean you will do exactly 15% in all areas. My experience says the ideal improvement to have '2X Profits in 6 months or less' is this:

No.	Particular	Figure	% Imp*	Revised Figure
(A)	Number of Leads	5,000	20%	6,000
(B)	Lead Conversion Ratio	20%	20%	24%
C	Number of Customers (A X B)	1,000		1,440
(D)	Average Sales Per Customer	50	10%	55
E	Total Sales (C X D)	50,000		79,200
(F)	Cost of Per Unit Sold	20	5%	19
G	Total Cost of Goods Sold (F X C)	20,000		27,360
(H)	Fixed Cost	10,000	5%	9,500
I	**PROFIT** (E – G – H)	**20,000**	112%	42,340

*Imp = Improvement
Figures in USD except numbers in rows A & C

[Table 6.3 : 2X PROFITS STRATEGY BLUE PRINT]

"I have made certain adjustments in the desired improvement in different areas. Basis my experience, for Small business owners to have '2X Profits in 6 months or less', these adjustments are much more practical and are easily achievable with 3 secrets & 4 strategies.

"Increase leads & conversion by 20% each (which is easy and later we will see how), average sales per customer to increase by just 10% and variable & fixed cost to be reduced by just 5%. 15%

reduction in cost seems not practical for many whereas 5% is doable for any."

"Wow! You've made the best even better!"

"Thanks. It looks that you want to say something. Is it so?"

"Yes. Though I am convinced with the *2X Profits Strategy Blueprint*; I doubt that at present it won't be possible for me to work on my cost. Do you think I would have left any room to reduce my cost? I have already worked hard on it and now it won't be possible for me to reduce the cost further – at least not immediately. What to do?"

"Haha... This is not your situation, but your perception of the situation."

"Meaning?"

"That means sometimes the problem itself is not the problem. The actual problem is how we perceive the problem. Your cost is not your problem but your perception about your cost & efficiency is the problem. Whatever I have shown to you in 5 to 20% improvement in 5 areas is perfect for you. You just need to work on them with a positive & creative mind. And I am with you for that. I will also guide you on how to work on these areas."

"Well, you might be right. But I don't think I will be able to improve on my cost even a little. What do you suggest for me?"

"In that case, you have to work a bit more in other areas and that too is quite possible. Look at the below table where I've considered cost as it is and improved other areas to have 2X profits:

No.	Particular	Figure	% Imp*	Revised Figure
A	Number of Leads	5,000	25%	6,250
B	Lead Conversion Ratio	20%	20%	24%
C	Number of Customers (A X B)	1,000		1,500
D	Average Sales Per Customer	50	10%	55
E	Total Sales (C X D)	50,000		82,500
F	Cost of Per Unit Sold	20		20
G	Total Cost of Goods Sold (F X C)	20,000		30,000
H	Fixed Cost	10,000		10,000
I	**PROFIT** (E – G – H)	**20,000**	**112%**	**42,500**

*Imp = Improvement

Figures in USD except numbers in rows A & C

[Table 6.4 : 2X PROFITS STRATEGY BLUE PRINT]

"Wow! This is something I liked most. This means I just have to work on 3 areas! That's it! But don't you think a 25% improvement in leads is on the higher side? Is it possible?"

"25%? Even 100% improvement is possible with the correct strategy. But let us keep it just 25% as that is enough for having '2X Profits in 6 months or less' with other factors.

"Before we proceed further, I must clarify for our friends that you must play with these figures, work on this table with your actual figures and see what is possible for you e.g., someone will say that Average Sales Per Customer is not at all possible to improve in his trade, then he has to work more on other areas. Someone will say that more leads are difficult, then he has to work on cost or price or conversion.

"First, take a pen & paper and prepare your *2X Profits Strategy Blueprint* with your actual numbers. Need not to mention, you can use excel/sheet as well. Think about what seems feasible to you and how you plan to double your profits. You have to play with the numbers – as suitable for your trade.

"After spending some time with 2X Profits Strategy Blueprint you will get an idea about what is perfect for you. You will be ready with a % improvement to get your 2X Profits in 6 months or less.

"Consider this as your 'interim decision' of your plan. First, let me finish explaining all these areas in detail. Do not take any 'final decision' on your *2X Profits Strategy Blueprint* before that. Hope that makes sense."

"Of course."

"How are you feeling now, Neil?"

"Curious. I am now more eager to learn details of *2X Profits Strategy Blueprint*[3]."

"The essence of strategy is choosing what not to do."
-Michael Porter

---

[3] *Though the term '2X Profit Strategy Blueprint' is coined by me (I believe); the strategy/process is not designed/created by me. This is already available on internet (in various videos/literature) and I do not know who is the original creator. I guess this might have been evolved over a period by various contributors – not sure though. I have added my own flavour by eliminating some points from it to make it bare-minimum & simple for small & medium business owners. If you are aware of the original creator; please let me know with evidence & reference. I will be more than happy to give the credit to the creator and my heart-felt thanks to you. We owe our gratitude to the creator indeed.*

<u>**WHAT WE LEARNED:**</u>

- It is possible to have 2X Profits without doubling the customers or without cutting a single penny from the cost
- This becomes possible when you write your business figures on paper – the way shown in the chapter
- Most businessmen don't take this pain and hence they don't get the insight. But once done, all new possibilities open-up for their business growth
- Instead of focusing only on having 2X customers; you have now five areas to focus viz: Number of Leads, Lead Conversion Ratio, Average Sales Per Customer, Cost Per Unit Sold (variable cost), and Fixed Cost
- The magic is, you can have 2X Profits by having only 15% improvement in all the above areas (figure may vary basis your trade)
- However, if working on cost reduction is impossible (though it is not), then you can improve 25% in Lead Generation, 20% in Lead Conversion Ratio, and 10% in Average Sales Per Customer (again, % will vary basis your trade)
- Give preference to table 6.3 over table 6.4. Go for table 6.4 only if reducing cost is impossible
- This is the most simple & easily doable strategy for having '2X Profits in 6 months or less' for a small business owner

#7: WHERE ARE YOUR LEADS?

*"You are out of business
if you don't have a prospect."*
-Zig Ziglar

"So far we have discussed 3 secrets and the *2X Profits Strategy Blueprint* for having '2X Profits in 6 months or less'. I am sure you have gained sufficient knowledge and you are thoroughly convinced to take action. Aren't you?"

"Yes. I am on cloud nine with full conviction & 360-degree learning."

"Fantastic. Let us move further. I will now elaborate one-by-one; each of these three steps for having '2X Profits in 6 months or less' viz:

1)   Lead Generation
2)   Lead Conversion Ratio
3)   Average Sales Per Customer

"Once again, I would like to remind you not to be under impression that only these factors are responsible for 2X Profits (or profits, for that matter). Certainly Not. There are many other factors which can increase or decrease your business profits. My intention is not to teach you the entire alphabet when what you need is just spelling. Basis, these few factors suffice to help you 2X your profits – and that too in a reasonably quick time.

"I also do not mean that these elements are more important and others are lesser. No. I only emphasize the point that being a small business owner – who is stuck with limited profits for the past few years – you won't be able to focus on all the elements simultaneously.

"Therefore, in the first phase of your journey towards making it big; you focus on these elements which will lead you to '2X Profits in 6 months or less' and then you can focus on others. Hope I am clear in my message."

"Absolutely. Thank you for the guidance, Mr. Profit. This is helpful indeed."

"If I ask you how do you generate leads for your business then what would be your reply, Neil?"

"I normally generate leads from walk-ins and then I have mouth-to-mouth publicity as well in my vicinity. I have a couple of salesmen who visit other enterprises and generate business leads for me. I also do pamphlets insertion in the newspaper sometimes – actually rarely."

"Yours was the standard answer by a typical small business owner, which I used to listen often."

"Is it? I thought I am different."

"Every businessman thinks he is different. We need to see things from a fresh perspective to judge it more precisely."

"That's a lovely insight."

"So, in nut-shell I consider that you hardly make extra efforts to generate more leads. This is one of the biggest mistakes most small business owners make. They do not 'generate' prospects but just 'wait' for them. In a market where there is stiff competition; one can't afford to wait & watch.

"Even if you think you can't 'afford' to do marketing or advertisements; you are doing injustice to your business.

"I often say to businessmen that *treat your business as your baby*. With time, your baby's needs keep on changing and you are duty-bound to fulfill it – irrespective of whether you are familiar/comfortable with it.   When your business needs funds; you are bound to get it else your business will die. When your business needs customers; just go and get them.

"Orthodox ways of marketing or advertisement (by the way, both are different but that's not the discussion at present) were print media advertisement, hoardings, banners, pamphlets, sponsoring a local event… etc.

"Technology has opened a whole new world of Digital Marketing for businessmen. Now you have a series of platforms where you can market your services/products with a wider reach and at a lesser cost. One of the biggest advantages of digital marketing is that you can control your ROI (Return On Investment) whereas it wasn't the case with orthodox marketing vehicles.

"Before I take you on a tour of various ways & means you can explore to generate maximum leads in minimum time; let me tell you something. Consider this before thinking of placing any ads:

WHO IS YOUR CUSTOMER?

"Clearly define on a paper who your customer is. Whose problem you are solving? Who is making the buying decision for your product? E.g., if you are manufacturers of plastic items for home use; you would sell your products to distributors in various areas or whole-sellers via your wide distribution network.

"If you are running a shop of readymade garments then whom do you serve? Kids, Gents, Ladies... whom? If you say that yours is an all-in-one garment store than note down all the customers (types of customers) you serve and you may have to place a separate advertisement for different types of customers because what is liked by women may not appeal to men. Therefore, be clear about your ideal customer first."

PRODUCT POSITIONING

"The next thing you have to be clear is your product positioning i.e., at what price bracket your product is placed e.g. whether you deal in essential goods, luxury items, running items, low-cost products, mid-rangers, ancillary items... etc.

"Even if you have a wide range, then decide which range or ranges you want to advertise? Because the language which will attract an HNI (High Net-worth Individual) client may not attract a common man. Your platform of advertisement and type of ads may differ with product positioning. Therefore, be clear on this as well.

"Now you can think of different tools for your lead generation."

SOCIAL MEDIA

"I need not elaborate on the widespread use of social media these days. Everybody is on social media. You can use this platform to spread your brand message. But beware, don't be pushy, otherwise, people will ignore your messages. Add value to your contacts. Give them something new, something useful, or informative. It could be a new idea, a new perspective, or can be your new product that solves a particular problem, an alternative way to do something... anything that generates the interest of people.

"Once they are positively engaged with your post, then you can pass a message that you deal with so-and-so product and how it will be beneficial for them to purchase it from you.

"If you are dealing in B2C (Business to Customers) segment and having a place where people come to purchase the products (shop etc.) then you can run a contest for them, which can be something like... they click a selfie with your product in the shop (or better you create a selfie point in a corner of your shop) and upload it in the social media by tagging your page. A person whose Social Media Post generates the most engagements (likes, comments, shares) will win. You can offer a discount coupon to the winner.

"People are crazy to have more & more likes & comments and they will keep telling their friends to do it and by doing this they are indirectly promoting your product or creating brand awareness for you – and that too for free!"

LEVERAGE INFLUENCERS

"You can take advantage of influencers for your product e.g. you are an automobile spare parts dealer and there is a guy who is a well-known YouTuber having thousands of followers on Facebook / Instagram in your area; then contact such a person to promote your product.

"You have to give him free samples and he may charge you for promoting. It is worth paying. When an expert says that the particular product is excellent, then people believe it to buy. It will cost you lesser than the usual advertisement and will generate more leads. For paying him you can have a deal with him on % i.e., rather than paying a lump-sum amount you will pass a certain fixed % on every sale through him. This is a mutually beneficial agreement, and a wise person would never say no.

EMAIL MARKETING – STILL NOT A BAD IDEA

"Though people say that days of email marketing are over; but actually, we are seeing a reverse trend. Email marketing still works provided the email is written properly and to the right audience. You may have to do some trial-&-error in this, but when succeeded, it will be like a lottery as it is almost free!

"With email; you are having direct contact with your prospective buyers! You can solve their problems, guide them, make them aware of what is new in the industry, make a special offer for direct buying… a lot can be thought in this area to make them interested in buying from you immediately.

"If you think from where you can get the email IDs then best you check your records if you have a practice of getting them somehow. If not, you can purchase it. Though it is more advisable to generate your email list; it will take more time which you don't have at present. So better, start generating your email list for future use and purchase emails from the market for immediate use (caution: follow guidelines & precautions of respective concerned authority/government of your region/state/country while purchasing & using email list or any contact detail).

DIGITAL MEDIA ADVERTISEMENTS

"Digital media advertisements are super-hit these days. Who is not on Facebook or Instagram or not using Google? Even we have heard that WhatsApp is thinking of starting an advertisement in its 'story' section. These are just a few popular names. You can check which is better in your locality for your set of customers.

"The best part is that even if you are in the B2B (Business to Business) segment, you can still use these platforms as ultimately it is people only who run businesses. So, they will be on social media or will use the Google search engine most likely.

"You have to critically think that where your ideal customer is spending time? On which particular platform you can locate/target him at its best? If you are not aware, you can target customers basis demographics on Facebook viz. age, location, profession, interest, what they like, which smartphone they use, whether they are frequent traveler, whether they are having an upcoming birthday/anniversary... the list is endless (check Facebook for latest update/changes).

"The logic is when you get this much detailed targeting facility available, use it to your benefit, and generate maximum leads. When you target the right prospects (basis your 'ideal customer') and you offer them superior products at a competitive price with an unbelievable offer; chances are very high of them buying from you. This is one of the best ways of maximum ROI (Return On Investment).

"Google ads are also a good option. You can use pay-per-click to ensure your money is not wasted. People dealing in B2B can use Google ads more, as businessmen are more likely to search for their buying needs. You can target them there. You can show your ads there.

"You might be aware that in Google ads you can show your ads to people – in defined geography – when they search for a particular keyword (or set of keywords). If you are not aware, find out more and take maximum advantage to your benefit."

HIRE DIGITAL MARKETING AGENCY

"In case you are not tech-savvy and do not have interest & time to learn digital marketing; even then don't let your business suffer. (Remember? Your business is your baby. You are duty-bound to fulfill its needs). Hiring a digital marketing agency is the best option in such cases.

"A genuine professional team will ensure better & quicker results than your trials-n-errors. Don't hire one blindly. Consult 3-4 agencies first, convey your requirement and ask them to give a presentation accordingly. After seeing 3-4 presentations and considering their prices, commitment & market reviews; finalize one agency.

"Be very clear with the agency which type of customers you want, how much you want, and by when? For that, be ready with your required number e.g., you serve 1,000 customers in 6 months and basis your *2X Profits Strategy Blueprint* you need to serve 1,500 customers to double your profits. Therefore, you need to serve 500 additional customers (considering you will anyway get those 1,000 customers as you were used to getting).

"Further, considering your conversion ratio at 24%; you need to have 2,084 leads, say 2100 leads (if your conversion ratio differs from 24% then re-calculate the number of leads accordingly).

"Here, also consider your infrastructure to serve. That means, suppose the digital marketing agency is highly experienced & effective. They can generate 2,100 leads in just one month, then think whether you can serve these many clients in this short period (i.e., 1,000 in 6 months vs. 2100+ in just 1 month!) Therefore, plan this out with the agency that how many leads you want and in what time e.g. around 150 leads every week. This will make your life smoother.

"If you think there is an additional cost (like an employee, or creating counter, etc.) to serve these additional customers, then you make that investment inevitably with no hesitation. This is the investment that will give you quick returns. In such cases, add few leads in your requirements (of say 2100) to make-up for the increased fixed cost. By considering this factor, you will make-up for your additional cost and will be able to 2X your profits comfortably.

"If you implement all these steps properly, any figure is possible to achieve, i.e., you can get a flood of leads – and not just 25-30%! This is so powerful. What do you say?"

"It is powerful. No doubt about it. But I have one doubt. Are there enough customers in the market? I do not doubt your strategy, but I am not sure whether those many prospects are available."

"Whenever such doubt arises in your mind; ask below questions to yourself:

1) How many similar businessmen are there who are dealing in the same gods as of mine?
2) How many customers they would be serving collectively?
3) How can I get these customers?

"I am sure, you would be serving only a very tiny % of total customers of all the businessmen in your industry.

"Therefore, there are enough prospects already available in the market. They are already making purchases of the goods you are dealing with. You just have to turn them into your business. Not all are having fabulous relations with the business owners. There are plenty of them who are ready to move for a better deal. This is comparatively easier than first arising needs and then selling them your products."

"Superb! You have opened my eyes, Mr. Profit. I must admit I had never thought like this earlier."

"Again, a disclaimer. How to generate leads is a very vast topic and my intention was not to make you Ph.D. (Doctor of Philosophy) in leads but provide you only the best suitable points so you can leverage on these points and make a quick move. Hope you understand this."

"Yes, Mr. Profit. You are so generous and knowledgeable. I am confident now that I will generate enough leads for having '2X Profits in 6 months or less'. There is no hesitation at all on this now. Thank you so much."

"You're welcome, Neil."

"We do a lot of one-night stands in lead generation and not enough in long-term relationships."
-Mike King

<u>**WHAT WE LEARNED:**</u>

- Lead Generation is one area where most small businessmen fail. It is mainly because they don't make whole-hearted scientific efforts to generate more & more leads
- Before understanding the tools to generate more leads; two points have to be clarified first in your business: Who Is Your Customer and Product Positioning
- Technology has not only changed the way we generate leads but also the quality of leads. Use technology to generate maximum numbers of most suitable leads
- You can use Social Media, Leverage Influencers, Email Marketing, Digital Media Advertising for generating leads
- If Digital Marketing is not your forte and you don't want to invest time in learning & doing it on your own, then it would be wise to hire a Digital Marketing Agency and get things done through them
- Chose the agency wisely and plan your leads as per your preparedness to serve customers
- There are enough customers already making their purchases from somewhere else. You just need to divert them into your business

#8: CONVERTING MORE

"It is much easier to double your business by doubling conversion rate than by doubling your traffic."
-Jeff Eisenberg

"**Lead Conversion Ratio** is one of the most looked-after elements in start-ups but this same element becomes the most ignorant one in small businesses especially when they have already made initial growth & have got settled. And more so, when the owner is relying on staff to convert a lead into sales. This is very obvious with growth.

"Many small business owners feel that their staff cannot convert that much business as they would do themselves. This is mainly because you are the owner and your employees are just employees. You have to train them on lead conversion. Believe me, this is the most revenue-generating training ever you can conduct in your business!

"Lead Conversion Ratio is even more important than Lead Generation. Because every new lead comes at a cost (we call it 'customer acquisition cost') but it hardly takes any penny to convert a lead into sales – except your skills & expertise.

"Refer our *2X Profits Strategy Blueprint* again (table 6.1). Just look at the first two rows (A & B). We have considered 5,000 leads with a 20% Lead Conversion Ratio (conversion ratio widely vary between trades e.g. if you are running a local stationery shop then your conversion ratio could be well above 90% and if you are having an electronic showroom, then it could be 25-35% or even lesser with increasing online purchasing craze!).

"So, in our example, you convert only 1,000 leads to sales. The remaining 4,000 leads are wasted. Now, somehow, if you learn to double your Lead Conversion Ratio, then? You will now convert 2,000 leads to sales. This is double than earlier. Congratulations! You've learned to double your sales – and by that double your profits as well – without generating a single extra lead!! Isn't it amazing?"

"Truly amazing!   I haven't thought about this before."

"You are not at fault dear. I am just emphasizing the limitless possibilities of this element. As said earlier, this may not affect businessmen like local stationery shop owners much as we discussed, but will certainly affect other trades & manufacturers and will more affect businessmen in the B2B segment.

"Let us see how you can improve Lead Conversion Ratio in your business."

WHERE YOU ARE AND WHY

"It would be a good point to start to know where you are at present in terms of Lead Conversion Ratio.

Just check your last three months' figures (month wise) and find out how much lead you got and how much you could convert month-by-month. If you do not have records then you have to rely on your memory that how many customers in the day or week you cannot serve or those who generate inquiry but do not purchase. You will come to know your Lead Conversion Ratio.

Lead Conversion Ratio =

$$\frac{\left\{ \begin{array}{c} \text{Number of Customers} \\ \text{to whom product sold} \end{array} \right\} \ \text{X } 100}{\text{Total number of leads/inquiries/prospects}}$$

(Pic: 8.1)

"If you are happy with that and strongly believe this is the maximum and you can't improve it, then leave the topic here. This also could be similar to the example we discussed, i.e., a local stationery shop or having a sole distributorship of a monopoly product in the area. In all such trades, your Lead Conversion Ratio would be very high as either customer has nothing to refuse or they don't have any other option. In such cases, you must focus more on generating extra leads (i.e., instead of targeting to generate 25%; focus on generating 60-70% extra leads)."

RESOLVE THE REASON

"In all other cases, you will arrive at a ratio i.e., your present Lead Conversion Ratio. Whatever it is, there is always a scope of improvement. Now find out why you are stuck at this ratio. Are there any apparent reasons for the same? e.g. it could be the ambiance of your premises, improper lighting or display issues or inadequate cooling or some practice which you follow but is not liked by customers or limited payment modes, your terms & conditions, your customer services... there are many possibilities.

"Genuinely find out what could be the possibility in your case. You may take an opinion of your experienced staff in this or a close friend who is a frequent visitor in your shop/office/factory/premises. Then improve that element. This will be a great service for your business for sure. Do it diligently.

"Once you have corrected that element or you find there is no such factor to improve then focus on your staff – especially those who deal with the prospects/customers. Find out the particular staff member who is good at lead conversion compared to others who might be not-so-good or average. Observe how he converts the prospect/lead into a customer. What he does differently than others or how he handles the prospect differently than others. Make that practice a standard process and replicate among other staff members."

> *"Sales are contingent upon the attitude of the salesman – not the attitude of the prospect."*
> *-W. Clement Stone*

"I have seen small business owners often hesitate & almost ignore to train their staff. When the staff is not trained then mostly his usefulness & efficiency will be very limited and he won't be able to add value to your business. Many businessmen fear *'what if I train him and then he leaves?'* But you have to think *'what if you don't train him and he stays?'*

"Training is not an expense; it is an investment. Improve the culture of your business, give proper growth to your staff, and don't be a miserly paymaster; he will rather prefer to stay & contribute more.

"As far as Lead Conversion Ratio is concerned, staff members have to be properly trained for the same. Training must include the technical and psychological aspects of selling. Staff must also be trained on basic grooming, courtesy, communication & manners. This is rightly reflected in how they treat prospects/leads.

"You may hire the services of a professional trainer for this. Try to plan the training in such a way that your routine business doesn't suffer much. If you have found one particular person having a very good Lead Conversion Ratio than others, you can ask him to demonstrate how he has been that effective!

"Let your staff do a role play in the training. Ask one person to play the role of a prospect/lead and the other to be a salesman. Observe how he is selling, where & what mistake he is making, where is the room for improvement. Repeat this with every staff so that all learn by doing. This can also be fun-n-learn activity. I bet; a whole another world will get opened for you. There would be many things which you would be surprised to know. If corrected properly, it will generate fabulous results in business.

OFFERS & DISCOUNTS

"Who doesn't love discounts & offers?

"Sales is not a blow in your profits. In fact, sales increase when you give offers & discounts.

"For better conversion, have offers & discounts on your products. You may play smart and be creative in making offers e.g. if someone buys from you today, offer him a discount along with a discount coupon for his next purchase by a particular date (this enhances the chance of him purchasing from you again within the timeline).

"You may offer discounts on bundled products or different discounts on different products (basis your profitability and eagerness to get rid of the item). This is a win-win situation for both – customers and businessmen. The customer gets the benefit of a discount and the businessman gets higher sales & profits.

"Whenever you make a wonderful offer & discount, don't forget to market it properly. Many a time your prospect is not aware of your wonderful offer. This is a pity. We can easily avoid this to a great extent by using various methods mentioned earlier in Lead Generation."

GIVE INCENTIVES TO STAFF

"Explore the possibility of giving incentives to staff on sales. Depending upon their job and your trade, you can have variations in this i.e., you may give incentive after a level or on a particular high-end product only. These are just examples. You know your trade better than anyone else.

"Formulate a lucrative incentive structure and motivate your staff to earn more. If staff is properly trained to convert better and they have a solid lucrative reason to do so, your sales will boom."

INTERNAL CONTEST

"You can also think of having an internal contest for staff. You may include sales performance as the parameter of the contest. This will generate healthy competition among staff and they will strive to win the game. The winner of such a contest should be appreciated in front of all and you can declare him as 'Employee of the Month' or 'Star of the Month' (or week) etc.

"After a few weeks once you notice that this is getting momentum and staff are putting their best efforts, then start giving award/prize. It could be anything that you think is justified. Better if you do it for their families e.g. the winner gets dinner in a decent hotel with family or movie tickets for family or his child's school books for free. When the family's happiness is involved, the person will do everything possible. You will be surprised to see their performances.

"So, these are the quick ways with which you can not only improve your Lead Conversion Ratio but will be surprised by the results."

*"Happy employees
lead to happy customers,
which leads to more profits."*
-Vaughn Aust

<u>**WHAT WE LEARNED:**</u>

- Lead Conversion Ratio is the most powerful but equally ignored element for business growth
- When business is settled down after initial growth and when employees take over to run the show, it is then when Lead Conversion Ratio starts declining sharply in small businesses
- Many small business owners feel their staff is incompetent to increase Lead Conversion Ratio
- First, find out what is your exact Lead Conversion Ratio at present
- Then, study competition, take the help of a neutral friend, or use your wisdom to find out what you can do to improve. Take those steps and re-calculate your revised ratio now
- Train your staff to increase sales. This is the best training to invest ever
- Introduce offers & discounts for customers to increase sales/conversion
- Incentivize staff for higher sales. Start a healthy competition among the staff and give a prize to the winner
- If the prize is for his family; the staff will go the extra mile to win the contest. This is mutually beneficial
- Not surprisingly, Lead Conversion Ratio is one of the most powerful elements to have '2X Profits in 6 months or less' because in most cases it enables you to double your sales without generating a single extra lead!

#9: GETTING EVEN MORE

"Get closure than ever to your customers. So close, in fact, that you tell them what they need well before they realize it themselves."
-Steve Jobs

"The next strategy to have '2X Profits in 6 months or less' is to increase **'Average Sales Per Customer'**. Rather than focusing only on Lead Generation and Lead Conversion Ratio, if we focus on how we can increase 'Sales Per Customer' then also our sales will be up significantly. Here are the ways to achieve it:

CROSS SELL

"Cross-selling means while selling A; sell B as well. If your favorite supermarket charges you for the carry bag; it's a cross-sell. You can easily cross-sell when you are dealing with products that have ancillary products as well e.g., you are selling paints in your shop. Then you can cross-sell brushes, gloves, etc. to your customers to earn more. Likewise, when you are selling readymade garments, you can sell other garments & accessories.

"If done properly, you can increase your sales at-least by 5-10% if not more. If you are thinking it is not possible for you at all (basis the items in which you deal), then wait. Maybe the next one is for you."

UPSELL

"Upsell refers to a scenario where you sell a higher variant than what the customer was intended to buy initially. Have you ever experienced buying a TV/fridge/mobile/cloths costlier than you had initially thought? That is up-selling by the seller.

"Up-selling helps to boost your profit to a great extent as it not only increases sales value, it most likely also leads to selling such a product that has higher profit margins.

"Suppose you manufacture bearings. Rather than offering a regular variant to your customer (or distributor); sell him a superior quality higher variant. Justify your offering with valid reasons and proving how it is better than earlier/others, how instrumental it would be in solving a particular problem better, how long-lasting it is, offering some discount, and making it a crazy deal for the buyer.

"Don't think you are doing an injustice to the customer. On the contrary, you are helping your customer to take an informed decision basis benefits, value propositions & durability of both the products. Your customer will buy only when he is fully convinced. He will love to buy from you again, as you are giving useful advice to him."

"Whenever you sell a higher variant product; you make more profits. It is obvious."

MERCHANDISING & DISPLAYS

"Attractive displays and proper merchandising within the premises provoke a customer to buy that product which he might even not have thought. Always have high-quality displays & merchandising in your shop/office/premises. It could be a cut-out, window glazing, illuminated displays, king-size screen, tempted pictures, crazy offer, the offer of the day, etc.

"Displays & merchandising play the role of an additional salesman in your shop/premises if used smartly. Be tactical in its positioning &

content. Again, it will depend on the goods you deal in. Explore the possibility and think about what best you can do in this area to generate extra sales & profits."

NUMBER OF TRANSACTIONS PER CUSTOMER

"This is one of the significant points to increase average sales per customer. Think about the ways how can you increase the number of transactions by your customer? Suppose at present he buys once a month (this is just an example; your situation may vary. Understand the idea and implement in your business as per your situation) then how can you increase it? Can you make at least 10% of people buy twice a month? And, if you can do it, then you have increased your sales & profits by 10% at least.

"Basis of your trade & situation, you may have to work hard on increasing the number of transactions per customer. Few customers will demand a higher discount, few will demand an extended range of products and few will expect better services. I understand that you can't satisfy everyone. But you can serve at least a few of them. Explore the possibility and see what best you can do here to make them come again & again for buying from you.

"When I was a kid, I remember my neighborhood grocery shopkeeper used to offer me chocolate whenever I visit his shop with my mom. As her child was getting free chocolate and he was getting happy, my mom started buying more from that shop, ignoring other nearby shops. This is a tiny but typical & classic example of how to increase the number of transactions per customer.

"The cost of chocolate was not an expense but an investment for the shopkeeper. If he would have thought to save the chocolate and not to offer it for free, he would not have increased his sales & profits."

"*Selling is really about having conversations with people and helping improve their company or their life. If you look at it like that, selling is a very admirable thing to do.*"
-*Lori Richardson*

<u>**WHAT WE LEARNED:**</u>

- The strategy of Average Price Per Customer speaks about how much customer gives you when buying
- To increase the sales value, you can use various methods such as cross-sell (selling B along with A), upsell (selling higher variant of the product), etc.
- You can also make your displays & merchandising your silent salesman. Use them smartly to generate more revenue
- Also, focus on how to increase the number of transactions per customer in a year. You can definitely find certain customers who can double or triple their purchases with you
- Small business owners don't find this element lucrative and hence they don't give proper importance to it but believe me, if you play smart, you can very well increase your sales with this

#10: THE LEAKING BUCKET

"Profit in business comes from repeat customers, customers that boast about your project or service, and that bring friends with them."
-W. Edwards Deming

"**Customer Retention** is like fixing your leaking bucket. If you do not do it; you are leaving money on the table. Without mastering this; you will keep on investing your time, money & energy into generating leads, converting them, and adding more to the sales – remember, you are doing this at a cost! 'Customer Retention' is the element where not only you can increase your sales; you can also save high on cost.

"In this highly competitive market; customers need to be cared, nurtured, pampered, guided, hand-holed, delighted... & what not! And why not? They are the ones who pay you. They are the ones for whom you exist. They are the ones who are at the core of your business purpose.

"People tend to move towards the benefits. People also would like to deal with people who respect them, who make them feel happy. Getting a clue from this, you can devise your customer retention policy.

"For having '2X Profits in 6 months or less' you may not have time & energy to work on all the customers. It is understandable. Basis, I have devised a strategy for you. It is based on the 80-20 rule. You must have heard about it, right? It says your 20% customers yield you 80% profits (this figure may vary depending on your trade & product). The heart of the saying is that there will be only a handful of customers who are most valuable to you.

"Find out who are your top 25% customers? When I say 'top' I mean who generates more sales for you. Now check how many of them are repeat customers and how many of them are just onetime buyers. Make a detailed list of it.

"Your next job is to meet all these customers personally (physically or virtually – as you may deem fit). Personally, means you will meet them yourself and won't delegate this to anyone else. Take a prior appointment and meet them. While you meet a customer; talk about his business, his life, his family. Build a rapport. Build a relation.

Please note you won't try to sell anything. Strictly no. Just build relations.

"Meet him again in the next 30-45 days. In this meeting, try to find out his needs (regarding your products). Observe from where he is fulfilling his needs apart from you. What is the total value of his yearly purchase in the items you deal with? Are you able to supply these items? Can you offer him a sensible deal for the entire lot? If you can crack such a deal, even with a few customers from your list, your goal is very well achieved. You will easily increase your 25-50% profits (or even more!) from these customers only.

> *"There is a big difference between a satisfied customer and a loyal customer. Never settle for 'satisfied'."*
> *-Shep Hyken*

"Even those customers with whom you cannot crack a deal (for various reasons – one of them could be they already purchase every time from you); at least they will stick with you for long, and that's an enormous achievement in itself.

"This is an open market. They also get offers & discounts from various suppliers. They also would have been offered better terms & conditions from some of your competitors. Possible. If you do not have a strong bonding with them, chances are high they move away from you quietly. And that would be a big jolt to your sales.

"Try to give some loyalty discount to these customers, if possible. And this is because they are your topmost customers. Check whether they are facing any problem while dealing with your employees or the business.

"If you have a few mature staff, you can also allocate one particular staff to 2-3 such clients. He would be one-point contact for their needs and you would be an escalation level contact for them (even in such cases, you will continue to meet them regularly).

"Next best thing you can do with such customers is asking for references. Do not hesitate to ask for it. But don't ask in your first meeting. First, build relations/rapport, then serve them better, then offer them a deal or higher discount or exceptional services, and then only you ask them for references. They would be more than happy to give it to you. Ask for at least 3 references from each such customer. Even one from each of them gets converted into sales; it is nothing less than a lottery for you.

"You must have noticed that this sole element is powerful enough to generate '2X Profits in 6 months or less'. If you think you don't have time, then you have to spare it anyhow. Refer to my earlier discussion on 'Create Time'. This is a golden nugget. Only a fool will ignore this.

"Neil, I have explained to you in detail how can you have '2X Profits in 6 months or less'. The way I have explained; you will be easily able to generate much more than 2X Profits in less than 6 months. I have given you such a golden formula that you cannot fail.

"Even if you feel that one particular element is not applicable for you or somehow not giving you enough results then you have other elements to push and generate more results. Though I was supposed to restrict my points to 2X profits only; but practically I have given you points enough for even 3X or 4X Profits!! Therefore, there should not be any reason you can't achieve '2X Profits in 6 months or less'. What do you say?"

"I am speechless, Mr. Profit. You have not only given mind-blowing ideas but have changed my perception of my business. You have broken many misconceptions I was having about the growth. Most importantly, you have thrown away all the negativity which I had for the market conditions, my business line, customers, staff, etc.

"You have charged me up with motivation, purpose & zeal. Also, the golden path you have shown to me is priceless. I am 200% sure my life will change. In fact, it has already changed because the biggest change happens in mind. I have already changed for the better & fine-tuned for 2X Profits. Nothing can stop me.

"I can't say how thankful I am to you for this valuable knowledge sharing. I truly believe that I am the chosen one. I feel honored. Thank you so much Mr. Profit from the bottom of my heart."

"God bless you, dear Neil. I am sure you will create wonders with '2X Profits in 6 months or less'. Best wishes."

"Your most unhappy customers are your greatest source of learning."
-Bill Gates

<u>**WHAT WE LEARNED:**</u>

- The final secret to have '2X Profits in 6 months or less' is Customer Retention
- You almost daily hear that 'Customer Is King'. Are you letting your customer feel like a king when he deals with you?
- Think on these lines. How can you enhance the customer experience? If you can do so, your customer will boast for your services and will generate more & more revenue for you. Then, the business will be real fun
- Customer not re-purchasing from you is your leaking bucket. Cement it well
- Spare time and meet your top customers personally. Build rapport, take a genuine interest in them, and have wonderful relations
- Try to find out what exactly their requirement is and how you can meet them in a better way
- Offer them some loyalty discount or exceptional services as they are your top customers
- Remember, if you don't do it, someone else will do, and then you will lose your customer (& profits)
- Ask for references from customers. You will be surprised with your business growth
- If you feel you don't have time for all these, then re-visit the chapter on 'Create Time'

THE WAY FORWARD

"Nothing will work unless you do."
-Maya Angelou

1. This is a book written for you to take the action and get '2X Profits in 6 months or less'. It won't happen by just reading the book. It needs to have your committed efforts. Have a re-look at your *2X Profits Strategy Blueprint* that you have made for yourself with your actual figures. Having understood all the aspects in-depth, re-consider your growth parameters in the *2X Profits Strategy Blueprint*, and take a final decision. Once done, now is the time to take action.

   Do you know why this book and the 'Rule of 2-3-4' will benefit you immensely, without fail? It is because of this:
   'Simplicity' and **'Minimalism'**. These have been two guiding principles of this book. Business per se is a vast subject and all the topics covered in this book viz. 2X Profits, Mindset, Focus, Create Time, Lead Generation, Lead Conversion Ratio, Average Sales Per Customer, Customer Retention... all are such vast topics that an entire book can

be written on each of them separately. But that is where this book differs.

I have taken only the most essential elements of these topics which are necessarily required for having '2X Profits in 6 months or less'. Moreover, I have narrated them in a very simple language – with no jargon or phrases – keeping in mind that every small business owner from all over the world can be benefited from it without any issues.

It is to be understood that this is not a book on Business Mastery or Business Expertise. A business has many factors than mentioned in this book. I nowhere claim that this is the best book for business growth. What all I have to say is this is the book which will definitely take a small business owner is in the business for over 7-8 years and feels his business is stagnant; to '2x Profits in 6 months or less'.

Therefore, I have carefully kept all such elements out of this book which is not necessarily required to have '2X Profits in 6 months or less'. In other words, if '2X Profits in 6 months or less' can be achieved without a particular element, I have opted not to touch it in this book – be however important. Basis, this book has become the *world's most simple & essential guide for having '2X Profits in 6 months or less' for small business owners.*

2. One thing I would like to share with my small business owners is: please hire talents. If you want to grow and make it big in business; start hiring & nurturing talented people in your business. Trust them, empower them, train them, guide them. They are your biggest asset. Though I have not covered these aspects in this book as was unnecessary for meeting its aim; I would like you to monitor it. And keep your employees satisfied. Keep them happy & smiling. Start doing this from the earliest possible. If you can transform your vision & vibration to your team; you will wonder about the growth of your business.

3. Always remember the golden principle of business growth: *'Cut the cost which is not adding to profit and invest more in areas where you generate profit'*. Keeping this in mind along with what I have mentioned in this book will change your business & life forever.

   I am sure you will implement the principles mentioned in this book with the 'Rule of 2-3-4' and will have '2X Profits in 6 months or less' for sure. With this, you will create an altogether new life full of happiness, success & prosperity not only for you & your family but your employees, their families, and your nation. More power to you. Best wishes.

4. Don't forget to **write your review** of the book on amazon's site. This will help me and also it will be helpful for lots of proposed readers. Please do it. It matters a lot. I would also love to have your emails for your feedback, queries, success stories, and everything which you share from your heart. Write to me at vinkr.ojha@gmail.com

5. All of you who want to learn more about this, go deeper into this concept, and see how it is implemented practically; you are cordially welcome to join me on my live webinar. Send me an email to show your interest and I will keep you posted. Please send your email on vinkr.ojha@gmail.com with the subject line *'Interested For Webinar'*.

As it is said, this is not the end; but the beginning. This is the beginning of your success, your turnaround, your growth, your 2X Profits, yours creating an empire. This is just the first step.

Happy 2X Profits...

- Vineet Ojha

"Many receive advice,
only the wise profit from it."
-Publilius Syrus

ABOUT THE AUTHOR

Vineet Ojha is a well-known '2X Profits Specialist'.

He is on a mission of *'creating 100,000 success stories of Small business owners double their profits in 6 months and live happy & prosperous life'*.

Vineet Ojha is also a Licensed NLP Practitioner[4]. He strongly believes that *'business is 80% psychology; 20% strategy.'*[5]

---

[4] *NLP = Neuro Linguistic Programming.*
NLP Practitioner Licence by Richard Bandler (co-founder of NLP), The Society of NLP, USA

[5] *Quote by Tony Robbins*

He combines psychology & business strategy to help ambitious & committed entrepreneurs who are having small businesses for over 7-8 years. He helps such businessmen to scale-up their ventures, make more money in their businesses, and do it FAST. Because *success loves speed*. It makes a lot more difference in business to beat the competition & grow as fast as you can.

- 18+ years of experience in Banking & Corporate
- Former trainer for entrepreneurs with a renowned SME training & consultancy company for Small & Medium Enterprises in Mumbai, India
- Former training head with a renowned trainer & speaker in Ahmedabad, India

Please feel free to contact the author through email: vinkr.ojha@gmail.com

"Entrepreneurship is living a few years of life like most people won't, so that, you can spend the rest of your life like most people can't."
-Unknown

SUMMARY OF LEARNING

- Market conditions or prevailing practices are not responsible for business stagnancy
- You need to update your knowledge & skills with your business's growth
- The force which runs a vehicle differs from the force which starts it
- What you focus; expands. So, decide where you want to focus – on problems or solutions?
- The profound, simplest & only 'magical solution' to the problems (similar to that of Neil) is '2X Profits in 6 months or less'
- There are some simple & powerful steps and few high-impact secrets to having '2X Profits in 6 months or less'
- Having '2X Profits in 6 months or less' is to be the first step to business growth for various reasons
- The master formula for '2X Profits in 6 months or less' is applicable for small business owners who meet certain criteria (as mentioned)
- This does not apply to solopreneurs & professionals
- This is also not applicable to those businessmen who do not meet even a single criterion (as mentioned)
- Remember the 'Rule of 2-3-4' i.e., for 2X profits there are 3 secrets and 4 strategies
- Secrets first; strategies second

- The first secret of Rule 2-3-4 is to have the correct mindset
- There is an altogether different mindset of a successful or growing entrepreneur vs a stuck one. We need to have the right mindset to move forward, else, nothing is going to work
- Self-Belief plays a vital role in a businessman's growth. It not only helps to have high confidence but also helps to have desired risk-taking ability
- Success is not guaranteed. That doesn't mean we should stop growing
- We need to stay committed towards our aim of having 2X Profits in 6 months or less
- Success is not what you get but what you become in getting.
- To make things happen for us and to have universal power in our favor, we need to daily visualize that we've achieved our goal. This is very important to have miracles in our life & business
- Keep your goal in mind 24X7. You will notice you are getting help in unexpected ways
- The second secret to having '2X Profits in 6 months or less' is focus
- Focus is the most precious element in this world, not even time, because if you lose focus; you also lose time
- You have to pay undivided attention to your business and especially to your growth strategies. If you have multiple things on your hands then your energy gets divided. As it is

rightly said 'how you eat an elephant?' 'One piece at a time'

- Having '2X Profits in 6 months or less' must be your # 1 priority at least for the next 6 months. If you give it the same importance as 100 other things in your mind; it's not going to work
- Your all decisions in business to be in alignment with your goal of having '2X Profits in 6 months or less'. Make it a mission
- Focused action is the next key to get the desired results. Everything is wasted if proper actions are not taken
- Ideas are worthless, if not act upon
- The final secret to have '2X Profits in 6 months or less' is to create time
- Time is to be 'created' because you are not going to find it any other way. You have to create it from what you have. Every minute saved is a minute created
- There is no point in learning the secrets & strategies of '2X Profits in 6 months or less' if you don't have time to implement them
- There is no point either in having '2X Profits in 6 months or less' if you don't have sufficient time for yourself, your family & your business
- You need to be more productive. There is a huge difference between being busy & being productive
- Do more in less. Create more impact doing the same work in lesser time. Learn to do things differently

- To create time, most crucial is to get rid of your routine business operations. These are either clerical tasks or non-revenue generating tasks. Avoid doing them personally. Rather, invest your time in business growth because no one else will do it for you

- Learn to delegate. You can't grow if you don't delegate smartly. Once you identify which tasks are to be delegated and to whom, then follow 5 step process of delegation

- Learn to work 'on' the business; not 'in' the business

- It is possible to have 2X Profits without doubling the customers or without cutting a single penny from the cost

- This becomes possible when you write your business figures on paper – the way shown in the chapter

- Most businessmen don't take this pain and hence they don't get the insight. But once done, all new possibilities open-up for their business growth

- Instead of focusing only on having 2X customers; you have now five areas to focus viz: Number of Leads, Lead Conversion Ratio, Average Sales Per Customer, Cost Per Unit Sold (variable cost), and Fixed Cost

- The magic is, you can have 2X Profits by having only 15% improvement in all the above areas (figure may vary basis your trade)

- However, if working on cost reduction is impossible (though it is not), then you can improve 25% in Lead Generation, 20% in Lead Conversion Ratio, and 10% in Average Sales Per Customer (again, % will vary basis your trade)
- Give preference to table 6.3 over table 6.4. Go for table 6.4 only if reducing cost is impossible
- This is the most simple & easily doable strategy for having '2X Profits in 6 months or less' for a small business owner
- Lead Generation is one area where most small businessmen fail. It is mainly because they don't make whole-hearted scientific efforts to generate more & more leads
- Before understanding the tools to generate more leads; two points have to be clarified first in your business: Who Is Your Customer and Product Positioning
- Technology has not only changed the way we generate leads but also the quality of leads. Use technology to generate maximum numbers of most suitable leads
- You can use Social Media, Leverage Influencers, Email Marketing, Digital Media Advertising for generating leads
- If Digital Marketing is not your forte and you don't want to invest time in learning & doing it on your own, then it would be wise to hire a Digital Marketing Agency and get things done through them
- Chose the agency wisely and plan your leads as per your preparedness to serve customers

- There are enough customers already making their purchases from somewhere else. You just need to divert them into your business
- Lead Conversion Ratio is the most powerful but equally ignored element for business growth
- When business is settled down after initial growth and when employees take over to run the show, it is then when Lead Conversion Ratio starts declining sharply in SMALL BUSINESSEs
- Many small business owners feel their staff is incompetent to increase Lead Conversion Ratio
- First, find out what is your exact Lead Conversion Ratio at present
- Then, study competition, take the help of a neutral friend, or use your wisdom to find out what you can do to improve. Take those steps and re-calculate your revised ratio now
- Train your staff to increase sales. This is the best training to invest ever
- Introduce offers & discounts for customers to increase sales/conversion
- Incentivize staff for higher sales. Start a healthy competition among the staff and give a prize to the winner
- If the prize is for his family; the staff will go the extra mile to win the contest. This is mutually beneficial
- Not surprisingly, Lead Conversion Ratio is one of the most powerful elements to have '2X Profits in 6 months or less' because in most

cases it enables you to double your sales without generating a single extra lead!

- The strategy of Average Price Per Customer speaks about how much customer gives you when buying
- To increase the sales value, you can use various methods such as cross-sell (selling B along with A), upsell (selling higher variant of the product), etc.
- You can also make your displays & merchandising your silent salesman. Use them smartly to generate more revenue
- Also, focus on how to increase the number of transactions per customer in a year. You can definitely find certain customers who can double or triple their purchases with you
- Small business owners don't find this element lucrative and hence they don't give proper importance to it but believe me, if you play smart, you can very well increase your sales with this
- The final secret to have '2X Profits in 6 months or less' is Customer Retention
- You almost daily hear that 'Customer Is King'. Are you letting your customer feel like a king when he deals with you?
- Think on these lines. How can you enhance the customer experience? If you can do so, your customer will boast for your services and will generate more & more revenue for you. Then, the business will be real fun
- Customer not re-purchasing from you is your leaking bucket. Cement it well

- Spare time and meet your top customers personally. Build rapport, take a genuine interest in them, and have wonderful relations
- Try to find out what exactly their requirement is and how you can meet them in a better way
- Offer them some loyalty discount or exceptional services as they are your top customers
- Remember, if you don't do it, someone else will do, and then you will lose your customer (& profits)
- Ask for references from customers. You will be surprised with your business growth
- If you feel you don't have time for all these, then re-visit the chapter on 'Create Time'
- Finally, 2X Profits will not be possible without your actions. So, START TAKING ACTION

"For a small businessman;

2X Profits isn't rocket science.

It needs only one thing -

Your 200% commitment."

-Vineet Ojha

Don't forget to write a review on amazon